IMAGES OF ENGLAND

AROUND UXBRIDGE

For as little as 6d a week-

YOU CAN HIRE *an*

ELECTRIC COOKER

IMAGES OF ENGLAND

AROUND
UXBRIDGE

JAMES SKINNER

TEMPUS

*This book is dedicated to the memory
of my parents James and Diana,
who were life-long residents of Uxbridge*

Frontispiece: A 1936 advertisement for the Uxbridge Electric
Supply Company. Their standard design cooker was quite a
modern innovation at a time when many households were still
cooking with gas. This model was fairly basic, but was built to
last – which it did. And for 6d (2½ p) a week hire charge, it
seemed a good deal.

First published 2004

Tempus Publishing Limited
The Mill, Brimscombe Port,
Stroud, Gloucestershire, GL5 2QG
www.tempus-publishing.com

© James Skinner, 2004

The right of James Skinner to be identified as the Author
of this work has been asserted in accordance with the
Copyrights, Designs and Patents Act 1988.

British Library Cataloguing in Publication Data.
A catalogue record for this book is available from the British Library.

ISBN 0 7524 3205 2

Typesetting and origination by Tempus Publishing Limited.
Printed in Great Britain by Midway Colour Print, Wiltshire.

Contents

Acknowledgements

I am particularly indebted to the *Uxbridge Gazette* for kindly allowing me access to their archive photographs, and for granting permission to reproduce them. My grateful thanks are due also to the following for their help in the researching of this book, and for the loan of photographs and other material: Carolynne Cotton and Gwyn Jones of the Heritage Department, Uxbridge Central Library, the late Peter Grace, Kate Randall, Lew Pond, Anne Twinn, Bryan Williams, Ron McKenzie, Mike Stoneman, Jack Dubrey, Ray Smith, John Laker, Patrick Burgoyne, Jean Hobson, Argosy Players, Theatre 7, Eric Bond Hutton, Tommy Thompson, Chris Wren, Lou Grant, Philip Sherwood, Reg Butler, Tina Hine, Fr. Colin Whatling, Wendy Heasman, Chris Berry, David Robinson, Barbara Fisher, Mieke Frankenberg, Ron Newman, Michael Craxton, Sylvia Taylor, Jan Ziegler, Frank Woodruff and to Ken Pearce for all his invaluable assistance.

Finally, a sincere thank you to ElaineVerweymeren for processing my manuscript.

Introduction

Lying fifteen miles west of London, just within the Middlesex county boundary, Uxbridge was known, in its infancy, by a dozen different names – all of Saxon origin. But they all had one common syllable – 'bridge' or the Saxon equivalent.

In time it became a place of many bridges, and obviously a place of many rivers and waterways. The oldest and largest of these is the Colne (once spelt 'Coln') which skirts the western and southern ends of the town, separating Middlesex from Buckinghamshire at Denham and Iver Heath. To the north and east, Uxbridge is bounded by the Pinn Brook, and even the Buckinghamshire river Misbourne flows close by the border with Old Denham. In around 1530, a diversion from the Colne became known as the Frays, while the Grand Junction Canal (later Grand Union) reached the town in 1798. The waterways powered several mills along their banks, resulting in a rapidly growing corn trade, which established Uxbridge as one of the largest corn markets in the country and guaranteed the town's prosperity throughout several centuries. After milling, the second most important industry was brewing, and by 1866 there were five breweries in the town plus a little matter of fifty-four public houses, twenty-four of which were in the High Street!

The seventeenth century was the harbinger of turbulent times that began when the Great Plague descended on the town in 1603, returning in 1625 and 1636, and causing several hundred deaths. The Civil War began soon afterwards, and a garrison of Roundheads was stationed in Uxbridge. Oliver Cromwell visited them in 1647. Two years earlier, the Crown Inn was chosen as the venue for the treaty that never was, and later acquired the misnomer of 'Crown and Treaty'. The second half of the century saw the continuation of religious persecution that dated from the Reformation, and many different denominations were affected. But the town continued to prosper until the nineteenth century heralded a time of change. In forty years the population had doubled to three thousand, leading to overcrowding and the building of dozens of small dwellings – in reality, hovels – in the many yards and alleys leading from the High Street.

Deplorable unsanitary conditions led inevitably to typhoid fever and cholera epidemics, giving Uxbridge the unenviable record of having the highest mortality rate in London. A third of the town's population lived in this slum-like squalor, and average adult life expectancy was thirty-two years. By the end of the nineteenth century, this figure had increased to forty-three years, and the town had begun to clean up its act.

The twentieth century was destined to bring even greater changes – perhaps more than anyone envisaged. The corn trade gave way to manufacturing industries, with many businesses starting up in South Uxbridge: the Steel Barrel Company, Bell Punch Company, and Uxbridge Electric Supply Company. Meanwhile, the old firm of Lowe and Shawyer was on its way to becoming the largest cut-flower nursery in the country, and Sanderson's Fabrics, which would eventually become an international concern, established their factory on the site of the Hundred Acres.

The First World War came and went, followed by the Depression, unemployment and hunger marches, but despite these setbacks, the 1930s saw many welcome improvements. These included slum clearance schemes (especially in the yards north of the High Street), new municipal offices, a clinic and a library, improvements to schools and highways, two new churches, an Underground station, a swimming pool and two cinemas. Several council housing estates were built, and advances were made in local transport. General rates were low, and with a quarterly season ticket, you could travel to Baker Street and back for less than a shilling (5p) a day. Uxbridge wasn't quite Utopia, but it was getting there. Then along came 3 September 1939.

The phrase 'Britain's Finest Hour' means different things to different people, whether it be Dunkirk, the London Blitz or the Battle of Britain, but Uxbridge's finest was undoubtedly the latter, because of the vital role played by the RAF station's underground control centre. On a momentous Sunday, 15 September 1940, Winston Churchill and his wife were in the plotting room as Fighter Command repelled 500 German aircraft during the course of the day. It was a day that proved a turning point in the war, and probably changed the course of history, as two days later Hitler postponed his planned invasion of Britain indefinitely, cancelling it completely a month later. The Prime Minister was so intent on following the battle's progress, that the trademark cigar in his mouth for once stayed unlit! The day's events also inspired him to create one of his most-often quoted speeches, 'Never in the field of human conflict was so much owed by so many to so few'.

From its foundation in 1917, the RAF Depot has enjoyed very close ties with the town – an alliance that was acknowledged in 1960, when the station was granted the 'Freedom of the Borough of Uxbridge'. The service has been 'instrumental' in circulating the name of Uxbridge around the world, particularly through the sound of music by way of the Central Band, which has been based at the Depot since 1920. Music has always featured prominently in the history of RAF Uxbridge. During the Second World War, the RAF Symphony Orchestra and Squadronaires Dance Band were in residence, and the station currently houses the Headquarters of RAF Music Services.

Since the 1960s, the name of the game has been redevelopment. The ancient, rural market town has gone. In its place a new townscape has materialised: a mini metropolis, dominated by glass towers and concrete structures of all shapes and sizes. Office blocks and shopping malls have replaced smaller establishments and corner shops, rendering the Uxbridge of yesteryear almost unrecognisable. Hopefully, the images in this book will serve as a nostalgic reminder of the way things were.

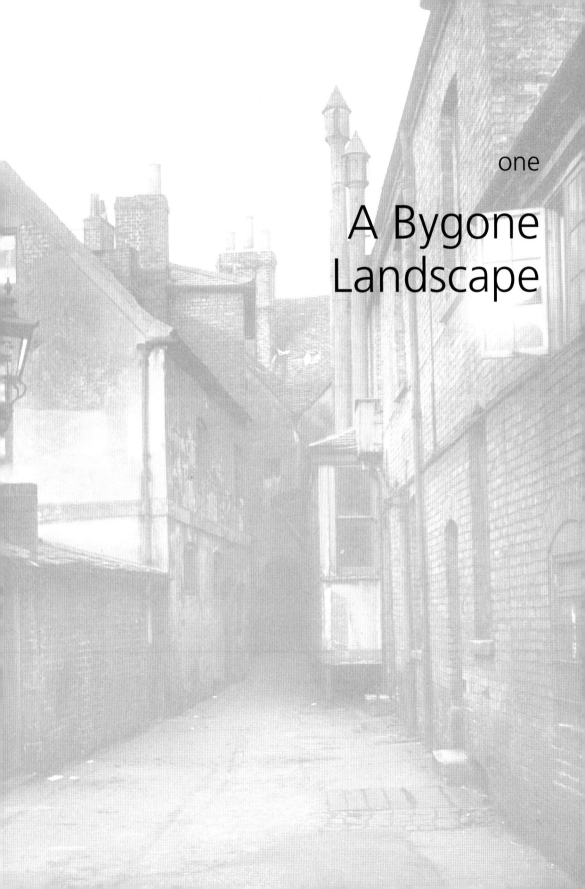

one

A Bygone Landscape

This picturesque rural location was a well-known beauty spot known as the 'Splash', formed by the River Pinn as it meandered through the middle of Swakeleys Woods. On the Uxbridge and Ickenham borders, the woods were popular with walkers and were a favourite place for black-berrying. In the late 1930s, extensions to the Western Avenue (A40) had made inroads into Swakeleys, and various housing developments in the post-war years have ensured that very little of the woodland remains. Not far away stands the magnificent Jacobean mansion, Swakeleys House, which was built by Sir Edmund Wright in 1638. The Lord Mayor of London, Sir Robert Vyner, who purchased the house in 1665, entertained Samuel Pepys there in 1666, and Pepys wrote favourably about the building in his famous *Diary*. The estate became the home of the Gilbey family in the 1900s, and had been acquired by the Foreign Office Sports Association by 1932. The house is now preserved by the National Trust, and has been used for commercial purposes in recent years.

The new concrete bridge built in 1947 over the River Frays is in an area known as the Hundred Acres between Uxbridge and Denham. This structure replaced the former wooden plank bridge near to what was called the Uxbridge Bathing Pool in the 1920s and 1930s. The river was clean and quite deep at this point, and facilities included a row of bathing huts and a three-tier diving board. It was extremely popular with the locals, and was also used by the RAF for a weekly bathing parade. It served a useful purpose until the Uxbridge swimming pool opened in 1935.

A quiet corner of the centuries-old common that played an important part in the town's recreational activities. Early in the nineteenth century, it was part of stag and fox hunting country, and the Uxbridge Yeomanry Cavalry drilled there. Later it was used for more peaceful pastimes, and Uxbridge cricket and football clubs both used it for their home matches. It was a favourite spot for picnics, kite-flying and rounders, and was also the ideal venue for the Bank Holiday fair that accompanied the annual Uxbridge Show on the opposite side of Park Road. In 1939, it 'did its bit' for the war effort when trenches were dug there for use as air-raid shelters.

The water tower on the edge of the common, c.1911. Built in 1906 on the highest point in Uxbridge, this familiar landmark on the horizon resembles a Norman church or castle tower. With water pumped up to it from Harefield, it greatly improved the town's water supply. The adjacent cottages have long since gone, having been replaced by more modern housing, and the tower itself has been converted into a private residence.

The corner of Windsor Street and Cross Street in 1929. The building in the foreground was the Uxbridge 6½d Bazaar, which was owned by C.Leno. On its side wall, it was advertised as 'The Cheapest House in Town'. However, it seems doubtful if the galvanised baths hanging outside were sold at that price. The shop featured a prominent display of billboards, including one for the Savoy Cinema that opened eight years earlier.

The junction of High Street and Vine Street in the 1920s, showing the Savoy Cinema on the right and Randall's Furniture Emporium further down Vine Street. On the left is a doctor's surgery which was demolished in 1935 when the entrance to Vine Street was widened.

Opposite: Grainge's Yard in the 1920s with its gas lamps, cobblestones and ramshackle buildings was typical of so many passageways in the town, although it was rather more respectable than some of those on the north side of the High Street. Running parallel to Windsor Street, with an exit by the Queen's Head public house, it still exists but is barely recognisable from this picture. The yard derived its name from an ironmonger, Robert Grainge, and dates from the early nineteenth century.

The main gate of Uxbridge RAF depot *c*.1922. It was originally the Hillingdon House private estate, and was acquired by the War Department in 1915 for use as a convalescent hospital for wounded Canadian soldiers. The Royal Flying Corps Armament and Gunnery School moved there in December 1917, and four months later the RFC was renamed the Royal Air Force. The building on the extreme left is the Camp Cinema, which was originally a lecture hall for new recruits – one of whom was Aircraftman John Ross. His real name was T.E. Lawrence – better known as Lawrence of Arabia.

The eastern end of the High Street at the Park Road junction in the late 1920s, showing the memorial to the dead of the Great War that was unveiled by Lady Hillingdon on 9 November 1924. The site immediately behind the statue was used to build the Uxbridge Methodist Church (Central Hall), which opened in 1930. Some of the shops and flats on the left were demolished in 1931, to make way for the entrance to the Regal Cinema, which was opened on 26 December that year. The War Memorial was re-sited in the Old Burial Ground, Windsor Street in 1972, and is now referred to as the Peace Memorial.

Hillingdon Village at the top of Hillingdon Hill, as it looked in 1930, with the church of St John the Baptist on the right and The Vine public house at the far end of the shops.

This early 1930s picture of High Street shops includes (from right to left) Sanders Bros Corn, Flour, Seed and General Produce Merchants, milliner F.S. Lindsay, and Frank Cooper's bakery and confectionery shop. Cooper, established in the 1800s, described himself as a caterer, cook and confectioner. There were dining and tea rooms on the premises, and according to a 1902 newspaper advertisement, he stocked 1,100 boxes of chocolates from 11d (less than 5 pence) to 15s (75 pence). Among his other specialities were wedding cakes and sponge fingers (for young babies).

The narrow hump-back bridge over the Grand Union Canal at the western end of the High Street in the late 1920s. The bridge dates from the early nineteenth century, and was rebuilt in 1938. The Swan and Bottle pub sign refers to the sixteenth-century inn, which was originally called The Swan (just out of the left of the picture).

High Bridge over the River Colne in 1930. Once known as the County Bridge, it separates Middlesex from Buckinghamshire, and like its neighbour the canal bridge, it was rebuilt in 1938. The road-sign at the foot of the bridge reads: 'Caution Drive Carefully', but appears to be irrelevant in this picture, as a pedestrian walks in the middle of a traffic-free road!

The approach to the western end of Uxbridge, as seen from the canal bridge in 1930. The GWR High Street Station can be seen at the right of the shops.

Another late 1920s view of the beginning of the High Street, seen from the hump-back canal bridge. The scene has changed dramatically from the other pictures on this page, as the road is jammed with traffic, which is largely due to the road works in progress.

A pastoral scene of old-world charm on the River Frays at the corner of Lawn Road and The Lynch, which was a favourite watering hole for local tradesmen's horses. On this September day in 1930, Leonard Kirby has treated his young friends Sheila and Patrick Burgoyne to a ride in his milk cart. Leonard, an ex-Royal Navy and Merchant Navy seaman, kept a small dairy shop in Chapel Street from 1923 to 1935. His milk supplies came from Provan's Farm at the foot of Chandler's Hill. This part of the river was also used by youngsters as a paddling pool during the 1920s and 1930s.

Horses and carts were familiar figures in the landscape right up until the 1950s. Bakeries, breweries, dairies, coal-merchants, and even furniture dealers all used them for making deliveries. One of the most common sights is typified by this 1929 picture of a council dustcart and dustman working in Cricketfield Road, which leads to Partridge Villas. The road still retains its name although there has been no cricket ground there since 1970.

A section of the High Street between the Market House and Vine Street in the early 1930s. A horse, probably pulling a brewer's dray, is emerging from George Street which led to the rear of Harman's Brewery. On the right of the exit are The Great Western public house, which dates from the sixteenth century, a newsagent and tobacconist that eventually became Young's, and a confectioners owned by Frank Voller.

United Dairies milk roundsman A.E. Willis is bidding a fond farewell to his four legged friend, Susy, a twelve-year-old mare, on the day in July 1953 that she and eight other horses at the Hillingdon Depot were made redundant. They were not about to retire and be put out to pasture, but were in fact transferred to other depots, which were not yet mechanised with new electric milk carts. Mr Willis had spent forty years with Express and United Dairies, and was quoted as saying he could not understand why horses that had served for many decades and through two World Wars needed to be replaced.

Shops that faced the Market House in the mid-1930s. Mac Fisheries on the left was previously Percy's toy shop, which moved in 1934 to the eastern end of the High Street, as the sign above the entrance to Bell Yard indicates. All these buildings were demolished in 1938 when the new Underground station was built.

Two new High Street shops adjoining the newly opened Regal Cinema in 1932. Another new building, the Central Hall, can be seen on the right, and three more shops were added (including Percy's) within the next two years.

The upper end of George Street as it was in the 1930s, showing Harman's Brewery chimney in the middle distance. Robert Lee, Beehive Manufacturer, was still thriving in 1977, having changed his business title to Lee's Beehive Works. Although his 'Honey for Sale' sign had disappeared, all the buildings were virtually unchanged.

A section of the western end of the High Street in the 1930s highlights the narrowness of Belmont Road before it was widened in 1936. The shops in the picture engaged in a game of musical chairs: the Chain Library acquired new premises across the road; Hoare's ceased trading; and Vernon Brown and Co. moved to the other side of the Uxbridge Electric Company, until both were demolished in 1971. On the left, Barclay's Bank, which absorbed the Uxbridge Old Bank in 1900, still retains its position, having been greatly extended in 1979.

The central point of the High Street in the mid 1930s, showing the recently modernised frontage of Harman's Brewery, which incorporated a pair of spiked gates from the original building. George Harman founded the business in 1763 and moved here in 1875. It closed in 1964, two years after being taken over by the Courage company. On the right is How's floor coverings shop which advertised the cleaning, dyeing and beating of carpets, in addition to selling them.

A most inconvenient hole in the road in the middle of the High Street, next to the No.607 trolleybus stop outside Woolworth's. On the right of this 1937 picture is William Coad's drapers and outfitters shop. The three Union Jacks flying on top of the Warren and Beck department store on the left are an indication that this was Coronation year.

A 1960s view of the St Andrews end of the High Street. The building in the centre of the picture is the former Savoy Cinema, which was by then converted to a bingo hall, its billboard proclaiming a jackpot prize of £140. All the shops on the right of the street were demolished to make way for The Chimes shopping mall.

A row of deserted nineteenth century cottages in St John's Road on what was originally Uxbridge Moor. Fronted by the grotesque shapes of stunted trees, they presented a desolate scene in May, 1939. But one house in the centre, which was converted to a general shop, remained open, and the Savoy Cinema billboard was kept up to date. The cottages were awaiting demolition, but this was deferred for a further seven years, due to the outbreak of the Second World War in September 1939. Then, in 1946, they were replaced by council houses.

The High Street looking west in the early 1960s. The gap on the left is where the once renowned Chequers Inn stood from around 1620 until it was demolished in 1961. That was merely the shape of things to come, as about twenty of the buildings in this picture met the same fate a decade later. The main exception was Barclay's bank, seen behind the No.207 Routemaster bus.

The camera has turned 180 degrees to film this shot of the High Street looking east. Buses no longer operate in this section of the street which is now almost completely pedestrianised.

A rooftop view of old Uxbridge taken from the top of the former main post office in October 1963. Buildings on the skyline, from left to right, are: the rear of Burton's tailors, St Margaret's Church tower, the Market House and back of the church, then Harman's chimney and brewery. In the centre of the picture are tobacconist Maurice Gent's shop and the back of the old police station, while the foreground shows the dilapidated buildings in Grainge's Yard with Laundry Yard on the extreme left.

One of the last pictures of the Eight Bells public house in the late 1960s. Dating from around 1747, it derived its name from the number of bells at St John's Church at that time. Situated next to St Andrew's Church and opposite the RAF camp, it was a favourite haunt of airmen, including John Hume Ross (T.E. Lawrence) who mentioned it in his book *The Mint*. When it was demolished in 1972 to make way for the relief road, the St Andrew's bell ringers sounded a last farewell, and erected the pub sign in their bell tower as a souvenir.

The impressive looking Montague Burton building which opened in February, 1938. It was like a Roman forum in appearance, and came complete with a dance hall and offices on the upper floors. Now there were four ballrooms in the High Street, the others being the Regal Cinema, Express Dairy, and Chequers Hotel. This 1960s picture of an almost deserted High Street suggests that it may be a Wednesday afternoon, which was an early closing day. The police cyclist is evidence that there were still 'bobbies on the beat'.

The Market House, supported by fifty-one Tuscan pillars, dates from 1789, and St Margaret's Church from around 1448. They stand alone like two sentinels guarding a piece of Uxbridge heritage, defying the destruction process to encroach any further. It is 1972, and the pile of rubble in the foreground is all that remains of the Burton building as preparations continue for the construction of The Pavilions shopping mall. Burton's was the final obstacle halting the march of progress on that site.

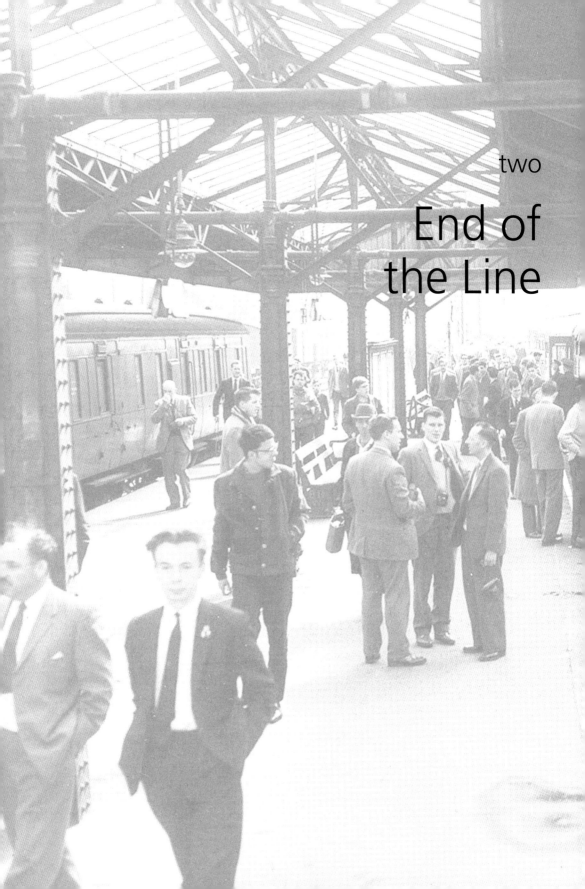

two

End of
the Line

A familiar sight at the GWR Vine Street station which opened on 8 September 1856. Uxbridge was the terminus for a 2½-mile long, broad-gauge single-track branch line, diverted at West Drayton from the Paddington main line. The track was converted from broad gauge in 1871, and was doubled in 1881. In 1904, the only intermediate station en route was opened at Cowley.

The shop and tea rooms attached to the GWR High Street station, c.1920. The station opened on 1 May 1907 to serve a 2-mile branch that joined the main line to High Wycombe near Denham. The overhead girder bridge was removed in 1922, after a scheme to link the High Street and Vine Street stations was abandoned in 1913. Passenger services terminated in September 1939, although goods traffic survived until July 1964, when the line was closed and the station was demolished.

A Vine Street 'through' train to Paddington approaching Cowley station in the 1950s. Through trains saved passengers changing at West Drayton, but stopped at all stations, taking fifty-three minutes for the run. However; in the early 1900s, some expresses from Paddington to Uxbridge clocked up a journey time of twenty-nine minutes. How today's commuters would love to travel to town in that time!

Trains passing on the up and down lines between Uxbridge and Cowley stations give the impression of a busy line, but in fact there were only thirty 'push and pull' services up and thirty-three down on weekdays during the 1950s. The majority of these ran only between Uxbridge and West Drayton, with the earliest leaving Vine Street at 6.10 a.m. and the last at 11.42 p.m.

A late 1950s view of Vine Street station from the island platform, showing a diesel two-car rail unit No.2A51 about to depart for West Drayton. These railcars had operated on the branch line from the mid 1950s.

The frontage of the station building on 8 September 1962. This was the day that passenger services ended, which was exactly 106 years to the day from the opening. The closure was due to Dr Beeching's axe falling on branch lines throughout the country.

This is not a bomb site, but merely what was left of Vine Street station after demolition in 1965. The office of coal merchants Burr and Gibbons, and ladies' hairdresser Maison Lucena, which dated from the early 1930s, are standing, although not for long. Deprived of rail transport to West Drayton, a queue of passengers patiently awaits the only alternative – a No.222 bus.

Seven months after the line's official closure, the station was re-opened for one day only, on 21 April 1963. The GWR Preservation Society had organised a nostalgic round trip excursion from Paddington, that visited the Brentford, Uxbridge and Bourne End branch lines. The pannier tank engine and passengers (two hundred rail enthusiasts) are pictured during a forty-five minute stop before continuing on their journey.

The first electric tramcar (No.202) arriving in Uxbridge on 31 May 1904. This view from the top of the Market House shows the tram in yellow and red livery approaching the Grapes Inn, on the right. A reception was held later at the George Inn, and public services started on the following day. The tramlines terminated at the junction of High Street and Harefield Road.

The former Metropolitan Railway station in Belmont Road on 23 October 1933. The first Piccadilly line train to arrive there stands alongside the much older Metropolitan train which looks decidedly dated by comparison. The station had opened on 30 June 1904, after the line was extended from Harrow, thus making Uxbridge the terminus for two railways, a month after it became the end of the line for the tram service. Eventually a much larger station was needed, and a new one opened opposite the Market House on 4 December 1938.

A trio of trolleybuses waiting at the Uxbridge terminus in 1959. These sleek, streamlined vehicles had replaced the old trams in 1936, running to and from Shepherds Bush on route No.607. A trial run was made on 9 November, and passenger services began a week later. The new terminus in the picture had been specially built at the western end of the High Street beyond the Odeon Cinema.

Trolleybuses 1854 and 1842 speeding down Hillingdon Hill into Uxbridge on 7 May 1960. St John the Baptist church is on the extreme right. Six months later the last trolleybus left Uxbridge on 9 November, which was exactly twenty-four years to the day since the first trial run. The trolleybuses were replaced by Routemaster buses; the route number changed to 207; and the terminus closed in March 1966. Bakers Road bus station then became the terminus for all routes.

Left: A 224 Staines to Uxbridge bus ploughing its way past the Van and Horses public house in Cowley Road, during a torrential thunderstorm that erupted over the town on 5 June 1954. The road was flooded to a depth of twelve inches, as Uxbridge experienced its wettest June day for six years. Temperatures dropped suddenly from 74 to 58°F and an average month's rainfall fell in a couple of hours.

Below: On the same afternoon, a former Green Line coach no. T.264, operating on the 458 route from Uxbridge to Slough, braves the floods in Cowley Road. Bus services to and from Uxbridge were inaugurated in 1921 by the London General Omnibus Company (later London Transport).

three

Sport and
Recreation

Uxbridge Football Club in 1888/89, displaying the West Middlesex and Henessey Cups
won during the season. Apart from not matching, their 'shorts' look rather uncomfortable
and the footwear could be best described as 'bovver boots'. This was the first time they had
worn the famous red shirts that earned them the nickname 'The Reds'. A decade later,
Uxbridge rose to great heights by reaching the final of the FA Amateur Cup on 23 April
1898 at Crystal Palace FC. They were beaten 2-0 by Middlesbrough who then turned
professional.

Uxbridge Reserves at the RAF depot ground in November 1929. The third player from the
right at the back is Jack Richardson, who captained Uxbridge Cricket Club in the 1930s.
From left to right, back row: W. Randall (secretary), J Robinson, W. Thomas, J. Moore,
E. Parish (referee), Jack Richardson, W. Rickard, B. Wade, J. Woodbridge (Trainer). Front
row: A. Pugh, I. Thomas, E. Goodman, H. Crookall, H. Cheater. The picture was taken at
an Athenian League Reserve Section game.

This motley crew took part in a 'Comic Football Match' at the depot ground in 1928. The gentleman in the top hat, sitting fourth from the left, is the Uxbridge entrepreneur and future football club chairman, Jack Hutton.

Uxbridge FC at the RAF stadium ground in the mid-1930s. From left to right, back row: John Barrett, Joe Barrett, J. Carr, J Povey, J. Smith, A. Akerman. Front row: T. Jones, A. Eggleton, S. Faggetter, F. Braisher, D. George. Uxbridge is one of the oldest amateur clubs in the country, and was formed on 3 February 1871. From the outset, they led a nomadic existence, playing first on Uxbridge Common, and subsequently on fourteen different home grounds. Since 1978, the Reds have occupied the former 'Drayreg' sports ground in Yiewsley, where floodlighting was installed in 1981. To mark the occasion they played an Arsenal XI that included three internationals.

Uxbridge Reserves at the RAF Stadium in 1948, having just won the Great Western Combination League Championship. Team members are, from left to right, back row: J. Watts, E. Williams, W. Greetham, F. Rees, R Thurston (captain), R. Williams. Front row: E. Roberts, D. Cheal, J. Taylor, G. Stubbs, R. Batley.

Uxbridge Minors Football Club in 1945. Team members are, from left to right, back row: Bramble, P. Dean, D. Hassell, C. Varley, R. Chambers. Front row: M. Dean W. Hill, H. Brooks, P. Stevens, ? Scuse, R. Margetts. Many of these lads graduated to the Reds' first and second elevens, and W. (Billy) Hill became a professional with Queens Park Rangers in 1951.

Having played on the RAF Stadium ground from 1923 until 1939, and from 1945 to 1948, Uxbridge finally acquired a ground of their own at Honeycroft in Cleveland Road. Their opening match was against Yiewsley in the FA Cup before a crowd of over 2,000. After a 1-1 draw and two replays, the Reds triumphed 3-0, before going on to beat several teams in higher leagues, including Wycombe Wanderers in front of 4,000 spectators at Honeycroft. This picture shows the team that represented Uxbridge in many of the early matches at the ground. The players are, from left to right, back row: R. Owen, J. Morse, R. Andrews, W. Rees, P. Poole, G. Sutch. Front row: D. Morgan, J. Poxon, D. Needham, R. Parham, D. Sheppard.

A happy Uxbridge team after their 2-1 victory over Hayes in the final of the Middlesex Senior Cup at Southall FC's ground on 12 May 1951. The players are, from left to right, back row: J. Morse (captain), R. Bennett, C. Silk, J. Beasley, P. Poole, G. Brown. Front row: H. Brooks, R. Williams, P. Stevens, D. Sheppard, J. Day. The team manager and coach, Trevor Jones, is standing on the extreme left and the chairman, Jack Hutton, is holding the cup. The Reds have appeared in the County Cup final on ten occasions, winning it in 1894, 1896, 1951 and 2001.

Uxbridge FC at Honeycroft on 26 January 1953. From left to right, back row: C. Smith, R. Nudds (trainer), G. Brown, J. Plummer, D. Dawson, E. Close, P. Poole, M. Pyatt, J. Hutton (chairman). Front row: A. White (manager), H. Brooks, D. Barratt, H. Brind, W. Lynch, J. Burch.

The Uxbridge team are about to leave Vine Street station on 22 January 1955 for a second round FA Amateur Cup tie against Alton Town in Hampshire. Captain Don Bevan is being wished good luck by Station Master E.C. Saunders, a keen supporter. A GWR 'special' had been booked to take the team and over three hundred supporters – a record number for an away game. Unfortunately the Reds lost 3–1, after being bogged down in a sea of Alton mud, and missing a penalty. Bill Chivers (manager) is next to the station master, and players include Hansford, Cartwright, Plummer, Merry, Brooks, Avery, Dunton, Egleton, Lynch and Brown.

Uxbridge FC with the Corinthian League Championship Trophy on 7 May 1960. This was the first and only time that the Reds have been league champions, although they won the League Memorial Shield twice. From left to right, back row: A. Odell (secretary), A. Taylor (trainer), D. Hall, B. Darn, W. Farlam, B. Dunton, W. Morris, Jim Taylor (manager). Front row: C. Brown, L. Frost, R. Egleton, F. South (captain), B. MacDonald, A. Dyke. Manager Jim Taylor was a former Fulham and England centre-half.

Packed terraces at Honeycroft in September 1960, watching as Uxbridge beat Yiewsley 2-1 in the FA Cup qualifying round. Yiewsley, managed by ex-Brentford boss Bill Dodgin, had recently joined the Southern League as professionals, so it was particularly pleasing for the Reds to beat their old rivals in this local derby.

A 1960s Uxbridge team at Honeycroft. From left to right, back row: J. Davies,
L. Cunningham, B. Caterer, E. Culver, B. Dunton, A. Ault. Front row: J. Etherington,
C. Brown P. West, B. Wibberley, I. Runeckles. In the early 1960s, a regular member of the
side was Derek Hoddle, whose wife took their young son to watch his father play. The
boy's name was Glenn, who became an international and an England manager.

Members and guests attending Uxbridge FC centenary dinner at the Bellhouse Hotel,
Beaconsfield in 1971. Among the VIPs along the back wall are: the President of the FA, Sir
Stanley Rous, FA Secretary Dennis Follows, FA International Secretary and Uxbridge Vice
President, Alan Odell, Uxbridge President Tom Try, Uxbridge Chairman Tommy Barnard
and Charles Curran, MP.

Peter Grace (left) who served on the Uxbridge FC committee for eleven years, receiving the 'Clubman of the Year' trophy from Chairman Tommy Barnard (centre) in 1967. On the right is player Derek West. Peter, who was also an Athenian League and Middlesex Wanderers committee man, died in 2003.

Former England manager, Sir Bobby Robson, is making a presentation to Uxbridge goalkeeper, Roger Nicholls, at a club annual dinner. Roger joined the Reds in 1969, and played over 1,000 games for them.

England *v.* Uxbridge at Wembley Stadium in October 1976. The Uxbridge skipper Colin Smith shakes hands with the England captain Kevin Keegan before the kick-off. The Reds twice had the honour to be asked by the England manager, Don Revie, to play the international team in warm-up matches. In this game, Uxbridge lost 8-0 against opposition that included Keegan, Clemence, Brooking, Royle, Beattie, Channon and Todd, to name a few!

The Uxbridge players sample the hallowed Wembley turf prior to the kick-off. The players in the front are, from left to right: Martin Johnson, Colin Smith, Gary Churchouse, and Roger Nicholls. Accompanying them and enjoying the moment, is the chairman Tommy Barnard.

Uxbridge Cricket Club at the Cricketfield Road ground in 1938. From left to right, back row: R. Keen (scorer), R. Franks, H. Dalton, J. Hollingworth, J. Fidler, L. King, F. Alford, T.L. Smith (umpire), W. Philips (secretary). Front row: N. Reed, E. Brown, J. Richardson (captain), S. Ward, H. Marks. 1938 had been a record season for the club who were undefeated in all their Saturday matches. Overall, they won nineteen games and lost five.

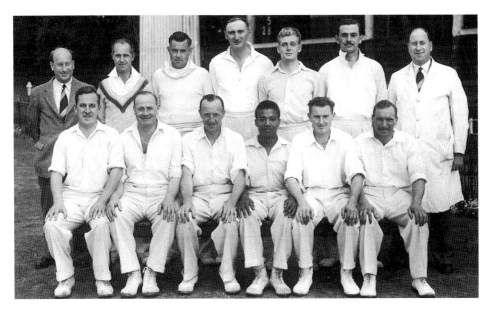

The Uxbridge Team in 1949. From left to right, back row: W. Smith (scorer), E. Brown, B. Flack, G. Knights, G. Arthur, E. Pomeroy, T.L. Smith (umpire). Front row: E. Yates, A. Marsh, J. Richardson (captain), C. Paisley, J.W. Ingham, N. Reed. Uxbridge is the oldest cricket club in Middlesex, and played its first matches around 1789 on Uxbridge Moor and later Uxbridge Common. May 1858 saw the first game at the Cricketfield Road ground, where the last one was played in October 1970.

Uxbridge CC in September 1957. From left to right, back row: T.L. Smith (umpire),
A. Baldry, E. Yates, J. Ingram, B. Holdsworth, D. Jarman, N. Reed, H. Lowe (scorer).
Front row: J. Wells, J.W. Ingham, P. Rundle (captain), M. Blumire, J.H. Ingham. One of
the best known cricketers of all time, Bernard Bosanquet, played for the club from 1902 to
1914. Bosanquet was the inventor of the 'googly', and turned in some superb performances
for Middlesex and England as an all-rounder. The cul-de-sac, Bosanquet Close, which is off
Church Road in Cowley, is named after him.

Uxbridge CC in June 1976, now resident at a new ground in Park Road which opened on
11 July 1971. From left to right, back row: G. Barton (umpire), R. Bishop, D. Browning,
C. Hawkins, M. Portway, G. Goode. Front row: J. Winter, M. Stoneman, G. Curzon, -?-
Thompson, S. Whitworth, A. Ruxton. In 1980, Middlesex played a county match at Park
Road, which then became a regular alternative venue to Lord's for one or two county
games each season. A year later, a young bowler, Norman Cowans, turned out seven times
for Uxbridge, before going on to play for Middlesex and England.

The Uxbridge team of 1985 were the winners of the 20 Over KO Cup, and are displaying their trophies. Since their move to the Park Road ground, Uxbridge have played in the Thames Valley League and Middlesex County League, while in their Bicentenary Year of 1989 the club completed a successful tour of Australia and the Far East The five-week tour was organised and led by the former captain, Mike Stoneman.

Members of Uxbridge Bowls Club at their Park Road green in June 1994. The gentlemen from left to right are: C. O'Connor, W. Marshall, S. Clark, W. Shannon, S. Panayi, S. Kemp, W. Williams, J. Rattue. The ladies are: B. Shannon, F. Marshall, J. Cope, J. Baker, J. Gray, D. Evans, P. Sparke, E. Tobin. The club was formed in 1908 by a small number of local businessmen, and the green was situated in the far corner of Uxbridge CC's ground in Cricketfield Road. In 1971, the club, following in its cricketing neighbour's footsteps, also moved to Park Road, where again its green is alongside the cricket ground. Over the years many members have attained County status, and Middlesex played county matches on both the old and new greens.

The finalists of the Uxbridge Chamber of Trade Tennis Tournament on 30 July 1930. This was an annual event played on the Uxbridge Tennis Club courts, adjacent to the cricket ground. The sight screens can be seen in the background. Records of the tennis club date from 1907, although it was probably founded slightly earlier. There were several hard and grass courts, one of which was graced by the three-times Wimbledon champion, Fred Perry, in the late 1920s. The winners pictured here were presented with their trophies by the actress Ellaline Terriss, the wife of the film and stage actor Sir Seymour Hicks, at a 'Flannel' Dance in St Margaret's Hall, Belmont Road. The tennis club moved to Park Road in 1971, rejoining their cricket and bowls counterparts.

Uxbridge Rugby Club in April 1994 on their Park Road ground, which they have occupied since 1992. The origins of the club date from 1948 when a team was formed calling itself 'The Borderers' with its headquarters at the Red Lion Inn, Hillingdon Village. The public house's red lion sign was adopted as the club badge, and the earliest matches were played on a nearby ground in Vine Lane. After many years, the club moved out of the district when a ground became available at the Belfry Sports Club, Harefield, and eventually became established at Park Road under its new name of Uxbridge Rugby Club.

Members of Fassnidge Bowls Club in the 1930s. The club was founded in 1928, and their green was prepared in part of the Fassnidge Recreation Ground, which had been created in 1926 as a memorial to Kate Fassnidge's late husband. Mrs Fassnidge had donated the land (covering six acres) to the people of Uxbridge and, when complete, the park included tennis courts, a putting green, children's swings, sandpit, paddling pool and an ornate bandstand. Not surprisingly, she was elected as the Bowls Club's first president.

This group of members of Fassnidge Bowls Club includes two long-serving players featured in the earlier picture. They are T.J. Williams (holding the certificate), and R.B. Twinn (second from the right). The others are, from left to right, R.W. Woodley, S.G. Nevard and W. Pusey. The club had just become the proud winners from the Middlesex area of the *News Chronicle* National Club Rink Bowls Tournament of 1957. Messrs Williams and Twinn are the gentlemen wearing caps in the 1930s photograph.

Right: An action shot of the celebrated Uxbridge racing cyclist, Lewis (Lew) Richard Pond. The elder son of a Windsor Street baker, James Pond, Lew helped his father in the bakery after leaving school, while all of his spare time was devoted to cycling. He joined the Uxbridge Wheelers in 1935 and the Polytechnic Cycling Club in central London three years later.

SOUS LE PATRONAGE DE
Paris-presse

Vélodrome
Municipal
▼

DIMANCHE
17
JUIN
à 14 h. 30

du Bois
de Vincennes
▼

LA PLUS
BELLE PISTE
DANS LE PLUS
BEAU CADRE

Organisation du Comité de Paris
de l'U.V.F.
●

REPRISE
DES
RELATIONS
INTERNATIONALES

Grand Prix
D'EUROPE
de Vitesse Amateurs

avec les Anglais HARRIS, de Burry; GOODWIN, de Birmingham;
POND et SCOTT, de Londres
le Luxembourgeois Lucien GILLEN; le Suisse Jacques LOHMULLER;
l'Américain Harvey SPIEGELHOFF; les Français RIVOAL, DOGUETTE,
DRON, CAUSERET, VIEILLEFONDS, LE GAL, etc...

Left: A late 1940s poster for the prestigious Grand Prix d'Europe race held annually in Paris. Lew considers that his best performance came in this event in 1945, when he finished runner-up to the French champion, Rivoal. One hundred riders from all over Europe took part in this 1,500 metre race, watched by a crowd of 40,000.

Competitors awaiting the start of the first heat of a 2-mile event on a grass track in Yiewsley on Saturday 22 August 1936. Lew (on the extreme right) won this race and the final, in addition to the mile event for which he received two silver cups and other prizes. This was his first competitive event and started him on the road to becoming one of the top cyclists in the country.

One of Lew's proudest moments is captured in this photo-finish of him beating world champion Reg Harris, who is nearer the camera, in a match sprint at Herne Hill in 1948. In the post-war years, Lew had captained English teams on many foreign tours, and won races in France, Switzerland, Denmark, Ireland, South Africa and Southern Rhodesia.

Another driving finish as Lew comes through the field to win a 5-mile scratch race at Herne Hill in May 1947. Among the many trophies won by Lew in a long career was the Lichfield George VI Coronation Cup in 1937, 1939, 1944 and 1946 – after which he was allowed to keep it! Lew also rode in the Tandem Sprint Championship of England in 1939 at Herne Hill, partnered by Jerry Burgess. He finished third in the first-ever televised event – a 20-mile race at Alexandra Park.

The 1948 Olympic team at Herne Hill. Lew is standing second from the right. Lew retired from racing in 1952, then became a pilot and flying instructor at Denham Flying Club. His first pupil was his late wife Iris, who had represented Great Britain as a hurdler. He still exercises and cycles every day, and for the past fifty years has spent much of his time running the Uxbridge United Charities Trust.

Local lad Chris Finnegan winning the European Light Heavyweight Championship at Nottingham Ice Rink on 1 Feb 1972. He beat Conny Velensek of Germany, on points, and on 14 October 1975, regained the British Light Heavyweight crown. Chris, who attended St Mary's School in Rockingham Road, became an ABA champion in 1966, and two years later, won the only British boxing gold medal at the Mexico Olympic Games. His distinguished career ended when a damaged retina in his right eye forced him to retire in 1976. Subsequently he was awarded an MBE. His younger brother, Kevin, won a British Middleweight title and on 27 May 1974 defeated Jean-Claud Bouttier on points for the European Middleweight title in Paris.

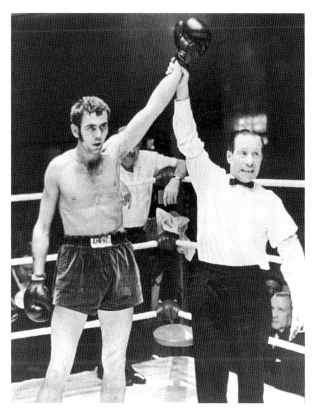

Uxbridge marathon runner, Reg Butler, passing through West Drayton in June 1955, en route from Windsor to Chiswick in the Polytechnic Marathon. This annual event, instituted in 1909, was started by Princess Margaret at Windsor Castle, and won by international runner Jim Peters. Reg's running career began with Uxbridge Athletic Club in the late 1940s, and later he joined both Finchley and Thames Valley Harriers. In addition to the Polytechnic Marathon, Reg competed in countless races before retiring in 1962 and taking up bowls with the Sanderson's and Richings Park Bowls Clubs. One highlight was running in a 2-mile steeplechase at the 1951 Middlesex Championships at the RAF Stadium – a race won by the Olympic champion Chris Braisher.

An improvised bathing session in the River Frays near Cowley Road in June 1933. Children had to make their own amusement in pre-Second World War days, and this was one way of doing it.

Even later, in 1951, the Frays is still providing entertainment for these youngsters deeply intent on netting 'tiddlers' by the Rockingham Road bridge, built in 1809.

Uxbridge and District Youth Organisations Swimming Gala held at the Uxbridge Pool on 17 July 1943. Swakeleys Youth Centre, who took the main honours, also gave a display of life saving. The runners up were Uxbridge and District Scouts, and both teams were presented with cups by Bishopshalt Headmaster, John Miles, and Youth Officer, Vic Sealy.

A crowded Uxbridge Swimming Pool in 1983 shortly before it closed, only to be re-opened and closed several times during the last twenty years. The initial opening ceremony on 31 August 1935, was conducted by the Revd Luther Bouch, then the chairman of Uxbridge UDC. The pool superintendent was Alf Price, who, at one time had managed the British Olympic squad. During the 1930s and 1940s, the pool attracted 4,000 customers a day, and in 1948, the Olympic swimming teams used it to practise for the Games.

Uxbridge and Hillingdon Silver Band outside their headquarters in the yard of the King's Arms, High Street, in November 1930. Conductor A. Sims LRAM, ARCM, holding the baton, is in the centre of the front row, and on his right is the council chairman James Cochrane. The bass player sitting on the extreme left is Walter Turton who had clocked up thirty-seven years with the band, when he died in 1931. Other long serving members were Jim Williams (second row, sixth from left) and Albert Holmes (front row, extreme right). The band was formed around 1890 and played a big part in local ceremonial events. After the opening of the Fassnidge Memorial Park, they presented summer concerts there on Tuesday and Sunday evenings.

The band at a concert in Uxbridge Central Hall in the early 1940s. Their conductor was now Harry Easy (extreme right, front row), and their blue uniforms were rather more elaborate with a lot of gold braid – jokingly referred to as the 'lion-tamer's uniform'. The personnel included many brothers: F. and C. Letherby, H. and W. Spurgeon, the Warnett brothers, and R. Roberts, W. Graham, J. Williams, J. Bishop, E. Richardson, P. Kemp, E. While, I. Trueman, and secretary E. Goodenough.

The band is about to enter a London and Home Counties Amateur Band Association contest at Westminster Central Hall in 1949. The youngster signing the register is sixteen-year-old Ron McKenzie who had won first prize as a solo cornetist a year earlier. Ron and his father had joined the band in 1941, and Ron's tutor and mentor, Charles Cooper, is standing second from the left. Charles was a member of the RAF Central Band and conducted a dance band for many years. Others in the front row are Aubrey McKenzie (fourth from left), Albert Holmes, Bryan Williams and his father, Jim.

The Uxbridge Band goes out of town to play at a fête in nearby Ruislip in July 1948. Leading the parade from the station is a guest conductor deputising for Harry Easy, and Bryan Williams and his father lead the front row. Ron McKenzie is bringing up the rear. The cinema in the background is the Astoria in the High Street. In the ensuing years the band continued to entertain and enter competitions at Westminster, Hammersmith, Walthamstow and Romford, and operated from new headquarters in a former council building off the High Street. However; its days were numbered and the end came in the early 1950s.

The Evelyn Warren School of Dancing from Hillingdon staged this concert at St John's Hall in 1935. The tiny tot wearing the star in the front row is Pat Read, and several of the older girls in the back row are pupils of Bishopshalt School.

Employees and guests pictured at the Uxbridge GPO Staff Dance in Cowley village hall in November 1941. The Head Postmaster, Mr Hunt, and his wife are in the centre of the front row, and the Head Postman, Mr Crown, is in the middle of the back row. During the Second World War, dances were a most popular form of entertainment, and took place at many venues in the town such as the Drill Hall and various church halls, in addition to the ballrooms at the Regal, Express Dairy and Burton's Buildings.

The forty-three-strong cast of Uxbridge and District Musical and Dramatic Society's production of *The Pirates of Penzance* fill the stage of St John's Hall, Hillingdon, in 1946. Leading players, Freddie Ashby and Jean Wescott, are seated in the centre. The society was formed in 1928 and, over 150 productions later, is now still thriving. Early stalwarts of the company included Harold Stoddart and Edward Moore, MBE, and later, Tom and Mary Bolton.

The cast of *The Boy Friend*, which was the first production of the Concord Society, at the Congregational Church Hall in 1963. From left to right, back row: Brenda Mothersole, Pat Howard and Jean Hobson (née Wescott) who founded the company and produced its musicals for twenty-one years. From left to right, front row: Derek Buttrum, John Wright, Olive Dean, Peter Dixon, Jim Sims. Jean spent four years at the Royal Academy of Music, and married a former Covent Garden singer, Alan Hobson. She returned to Uxbridge Musical Society, directing their shows for fourteen years, before forming a new group Pastiche Theatre, in 1997.

A scene from Argosy Players' first production, *A Midsummer Night's Dream* at St John's Hall, Hillingdon in May, 1947. Bernard Marriott and Marion Lane as Oberon and Titania take centre stage with the fairies, some of whom were played by members' children. The co-producers were Kit Beavan and Marion Lane. Argosy was a spin-off from the Old Uxonians' Drama Section, and the founder members included Tom Barnard, Charles Glover and the three mentioned above. The group, which continues to provide a variety of entertainment including drama, pantomime and musicals, will celebrate its fifty-seventh anniversary in 2004.

Argosy's presentation of *Hamlet* at St John's Hall, in May 1957, showing Ronald Cousins as the King and Trevor Bell as Laertes. Hamlet was played by Tom Barnard. A few days earlier, the group had performed the play at the Civic Theatre, Southwark, as part of a festival, to which they were invited several years running.

A scene from the Theatre 7 Group's production of *A View From The Bridge* at Uxbridge Technical College in October 1970. The company was formed in 1969 by Michael and Audrey Skinner, together with five other members – hence the name Theatre 7. Since then, the group has staged a total of fifty-eight productions at various venues including St John's Hall, Beck Theatre and Compass Theatre.

The cast and backstage crew of *Lord Arthur Savile's Crime* presented by Theatre 7 at the Compass Theatre in October 1996. From left to right, standing: S. Crossley, A. Wicking, M. Skinner, P. Page, C. Quaif, V. Drewett, S. Green, B. Twinn, P. Long. Sitting: V. Reilly, A. Skinner, J. Quaif, A. Twinn, R. Ray.

Mrs Adela (Addie) Harrison is in front of what was Uxbridge's first cinema, Rockingham Hall, in the Lynch. Adela's father, Jack Hutton, opened the hall (which is now converted into offices) on 6 August 1910, before moving upmarket when he acquired the larger Empire Electric in Vine Street a year later. The Empire survived until 1932, when it was purchased by the council and converted into a fire station in 1933.

The Savoy Cinema on the corner of High Street and Vine Street, after its conversion to a bingo hall. Built on the site of the old town hall, the cinema opened on 3 October 1921 and closed on 10 June 1960. It survived a German bomb on the roof in November 1940, but could not cope with falling attendances. The building was demolished in May 1983, and the Royal Bank of Scotland now occupies the site.

Left: Stanley Winchester, the last commissionaire to be employed by the Regal cinema, locks the front doors after the last screening on 4 November 1977. The Regal opened on 26 December 1931 and after closure remained empty for seven years, before re-opening as a snooker hall and night club in 1984.

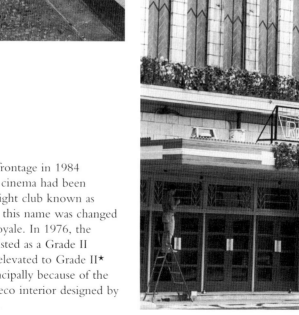

Right: The Regal frontage in 1984 indicating that the cinema had been converted into a night club known as Regals. Eventually this name was changed to Discotheque Royale. In 1976, the cinema had been listed as a Grade II building, and was elevated to Grade II★ status in 2000, principally because of the magnificent Art Deco interior designed by E. Norman Bailey.

The Odeon Cinema in 1981, a year before it closed. Built on the site of the former Brookfield Hotel at the western end of the High Street, the Odeon opened on 20 June 1938 in a blaze of glory with a special preview of *The Drum*, attended by Sabu, Valerie Hobson, Anna Neagle, Herbert Wilcox, and Odeon chief Oscar Deutsch. It was 'tripled' in 1976, and demolished in 1984. Then in 1990 a smaller two-screen Odeon was built on the same site.

Sarah van de Burgh (of *Neighbours* fame) flanked by US marines, attending a gala night at the latest Uxbridge Odeon on 8 March 2001. The new nine screen multiplex, situated within the Chimes shopping mall, opened to the general public on the following day.

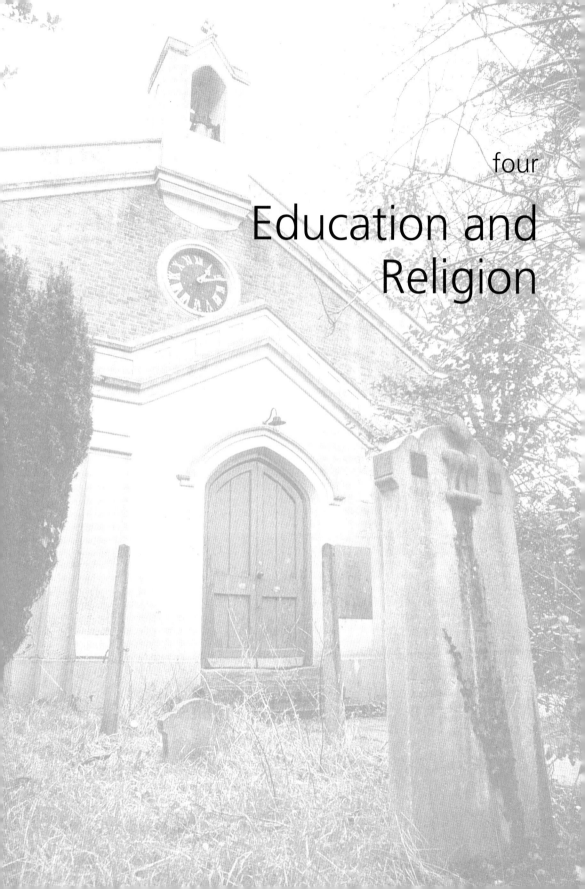

four

Education and Religion

The sixth form at Uxbridge County School in The Greenway, *c*.1923, with teacher Miss Hutton on the extreme right. The pupil on the extreme left is the future actor Bernard Miles. The school opened in September 1907 – the year that Bernard was born – and consisted of six classrooms, an assembly hall, science laboratory and a cookery and manual training centre.

The County School's Town House football team of 1924/5. Bernard Miles is on the extreme left of the front row and his older brother Leonard is in the centre holding the ball.

When the County School became overcrowded in 1928, it moved to new premises in Hillingdon Village. The old building then became known as the Greenway Central Senior School to accommodate pupils from the age of eleven upwards after they left the local elementary (or junior) schools. A new block had been added and the picture shows the official opening on 24 November 1928, by Sir John Gilbert KBE, chairman of the London Education Committee. Also present were council chairman James Cochrane, Revd Luther Bouch, county alderman H.S. Button and headmaster H.W. Beagley. The assembled scholars sang a selection of sea shanties in between the speeches.

Greenway School in 1983, showing that very little had changed since its days as the County School in the 1920s.

The County School's new premises in Royal Lane, Hillingdon, which opened in October 1928. Two years later it was renamed Bishopshalt and acquired its own coat of arms. The mansion was built in 1858, but derives its name from earlier times, when the Bishops of Worcester, who owned the site, halted there on their journeys to and from London.

Bishopshalt Sports Day, 1931. Here the chairman of the governors, Mr (later Sir) Cecil Fane de Salis, addresses pupils at the prize-giving ceremony. Headmaster John Miles, who served from 1929 to 1948, is sitting at the desk on the left. Note the sea of distinctive Bishopshalt caps in the foreground.

The school's first musical production, *The Mikado*, staged across the road at St John's Hall in December 1936. From left to right, back row: C. Hutchings, L. Clarke, B. Butler, W. Jackson, E. Williams, W. Kennedy. Front row: M. Gale, M. Polwart, B. Tapping. The cast was made up of pupils, teachers and old scholars.

The Bishopshalt girls hockey team of 1938. From left to right, back row: M. Bridgeland, B. Tapping, M. Curtis, M. Minns, R. Smith, M. Chaney. Front row: J. Suttle, E. Pizzey, J. Morris, K. Pizzey, J. Fitzen.

Left: Pupils of Form 5c at Bishopshalt in July 1945. From left to right, front row: John Hare, Margaret James, Eileen Dobner, Josephine Lunn. Second row: Alan Taylor, Philip Sherwood, Ken Swann, Allan Peachey. Third row: Violet Seal, Joan Harvey, Patricia Clamp, Pamela Lambert, Doreen Hardwick, Peggy Bewley. Fourth row: Pamela Bunting, Ann Wood, Thelma Adams, Phyllis Somers, Beryl Tombs, Patricia Pocock. Fifth row: Michael Golden, Adam Abbott, Stanley Parslow, M. Parks (form master), Peter Fuller, Pamela Hide. Back row: Roy Green, Leonard Harris.

Below: First year sixth-form girls at Bishopshalt in 1946. From left to right, front row: Pamela Haynes, Valerie Caradine, Pamela Bunting, Peggy Trim, Janet Holloway. Second row: Hilda Wilson, Carol Payne, -?-, Norma Rowe, Ann Wood. Back row: Patricia Pocock, Pamela Lambert.

A second-form netball match at the school in 1977. From left to right the players are: Sandra Sculley, Sharan West, Jane Morris, Julie Hudson, Tina Clark, Sonia Curtis, Jean Hunt, Deborah Robinson.

A happy group of Bishopshalt old scholars assembled in front of the school on 12 October 1996. They were the 'class of 1946', celebrating a fiftieth anniversary reunion. The event was organised by former head girl (in 1952) Shirley Davies (née Stears), with the help of her former classmate, Clive Brown. Another ex-pupil and teacher, Ken Pearce, organised an exhibition of 1946 photographs for the occasion.

St John's (C of E) School in St John's Road, formerly Uxbridge Moor. Dating from 1843, the school closed at the end of July 1980. Later, the building was used for commercial purposes.

Pupils of St Andrew's School with their teachers in the early 1930s. The lads had every reason to look pleased with themselves, having just been selected as 'Wembley Ball Boys' to do duty at the famous stadium.

St Mary's Roman Catholic Junior School in Rockingham Road. The school opened on 24 February 1895, for pupils up to the age of fourteen. It was considerably extended in 1937, when three new classrooms were added. The school built a new assembly hall, kitchens and a nursery school during the 1970s.

A group of smiling faces in the St Mary's playground during the summer of 1937. Sitting next to a visiting priest is teacher Molly Smith (later Mrs Duffy) who taught at the school from 1934 to 1962. The headmistress at the time, Miss Elizabeth Hoey, served even longer, from 1918 to 1954.

Pupils of Whitehall School, Cowley Road, in 1935. The junior school opened in October 1911, and was divided into junior and infant sections in 1928. Further buildings were added during the 1960s. One long-serving teacher at Whitehall was Miss Dorothy Hillier, who taught from 1927 to 1966.

In February 1997, the Whitehall pupils were producing their own newspaper. (Computer technology was not available in 1935.) The paper was produced during six sessions of their weekly lunchtime newspaper club, and then entered in a competition organised by *The Daily Telegraph*. Copies of the *Gazette* are purely coincidental!

Uxbridge Technical College, Park Road, in the 1970s. The college opened in 1965, and has continued to expand ever since. It has now been renamed Uxbridge College.

Students crossing the campus of Brunel University in 1995. The university was built on the vast expanse of land vacated by the Lowe and Shawyer nurseries after that company went into voluntary liquidation in 1958. The former Uxbridge football ground, Honeycroft, and a stretch of GWR line from Cowley to The Greenway are also part of the site. Appropriately enough, the university is named after the GWR's most famous engineer, Isambard Kingdom Brunel. The first buildings were erected in 1965, with the first students arriving in 1966.

The Church of St John the Baptist on Hillingdon Hill. Dating from Saxon times, this Hillingdon parish church became the mother church to many others in the area. It was restored in 1847-1848, and the interior still retains some sixteenth-century brasses and post-Reformation monuments. The tower was built in 1629.

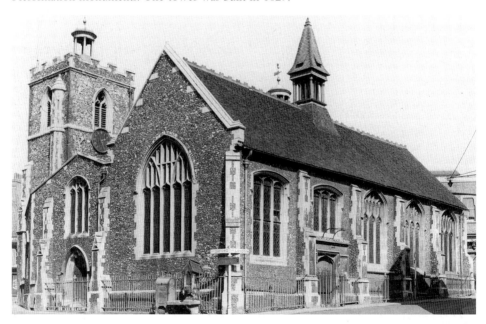

St Margaret's Church in Windsor Street began life as a chapel of ease to St John's in around 1200. The earliest parts of the present structure date from 1447, and restorations took place in 1820 and 1872. During the 1920s and 1930s, the area outside the south aisle became known as 'Speakers Corner', when used as a political platform on Saturday nights by members of various parties, one of whom was the Fascist leader Oswald Mosley.

St Andrew's Church at the eastern end of Uxbridge High Street. The church was designed by Sir George Gilbert Scott, and built by local builders, Fassnidge and Son, using bricks made in Cowley. It opened in 1865 with its own parish. Its dominating feature is a stately 150ft high spire, which received a mention in T.E. Lawrence's book *The Mint*.

St Peter's Church in The Greenway was dedicated as a mission church of St Andrew's in 1906. Church of England services continued here until the 1980s, after which the building was used for community work, and named Uxbridge Centre.

The Friends Meeting House, Friends Walk, near Belmont Road. The Society of Friends, or Quakers, have held meetings in Uxbridge since 1658. Their first purpose-built meeting house was erected in 1692, being replaced in 1818 by the present building seen in the picture.

Uxbridge Methodist Church (Central Hall) in Park Road, in 1983, two years before it was demolished. This impressive building opened in 1930, and as it could seat 750 people, it was frequently used for public meetings, orchestral and choral concerts, in addition to religious services.

The church of St John the Evangelist in St John's Road, Uxbridge Moor. It was built in 1838, and was detached from the mother parish of Hillingdon in 1842. It is believed to have been sited on the Moor as a steadying influence on an apparently lawless neighbourhood. This picture, taken in 1998, shows it in a somewhat derelict condition five years after it had been closed as a place of worship.

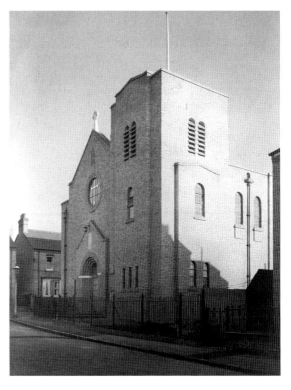

The church of Our Lady of Lourdes and St Michael, Bassett Road, prior to its opening in 1931. This new Roman Catholic church replaced a corrugated iron building in Lawn Road that had been established by West Drayton priest Fr Michael Wren on 29 September 1892. During the 1940s, many well-known film actors attended services here, including Mary Morris (*The Thief of Bagdad* and *Pimpernel Smith*) Finlay Currie (*49th Parallel* and *Great Expectations*) and Noel Purcell (*The Blue Lagoon*). Most of the neighbouring properties were demolished during the Uxbridge redevelopment scheme of 1969-1970, but the church still stands in splendid isolation on what is virtually an island site.

Montague Hall, George Street, the headquarters of the Salvation Army from 1898 until 1971. The Uxbridge Corps was formed in 1887, and its first home was Jubilee Hall in Bell Yard.

On a wet Saturday, 2 November 1974, the 'Army' makes its traditional March of Witness along Windsor Street to its new purpose-built base in Cowley Road. Since leaving Montague Hall, the Salvationists had occupied temporary quarters in the former Cowley Road school and the Central Hall.

five

Public
Services

The Uxbridge Volunteer Fire Brigade at their Windsor Street headquarters, *c*.1890. The brigade was established in 1865 and made up of dedicated amateurs. For many years they relied on horse-drawn engines and, until the early twentieth century, made a call-out charge for their services.

The new fire station in Cricketfield Road, to which the Brigade moved in 1909. It was a year after the death of their much-respected chief officer, Ben Gales, who held that position for thirty years. Much of the building still exists, and is part of Randall's premises.

Three members of the brigade proudly displaying a new engine, christened 'Greyhound' by Mrs Howard Button on 7 January 1935. Now fully mechanised, the brigade had another new fire station (seen in the picture) in Vine Street. This building was the old Empire Electric cinema, which was converted in 1933.

Uxbridge firemen taking a day off from fire-fighting as they parade in front of the new fire station with the GWR station in the background. They are waiting to take part in a procession celebrating the Silver Jubilee of King George V in May 1935. They appear to have shown great ingenuity in choosing their array of costumes and, judging by some of the banners on their cart, a wicked sense of humour!

Left: Fountain's Mill, built in the early nineteenth century, and one of four powered by the River Frays, was the scene of one of the biggest fires attended by the Uxbridge Brigade. In fact, six other brigades were called on 12 May 1954, when firemen fought 30ft high flames for almost three hours. The picture shows Wembley fireman D. Sollowan directing a jet from a 100ft high turntable ladder. The mill, at the western end of the High Street, suffered severe damage, and what remained of the building is now an Adult Training Centre.

Below: Long before the days of 'lollipop' women, local 'bobbies' undertook a variety of tasks. Here the gentle arm of the law guides a party of children from St Andrew's school across the High Street in 1928.

Right: Liberals and Conservatives join forces outside Windsor Street police station on 17 June 1978, collecting signatures on a petition to keep the station open. On the same day, a demonstration took place in the town centre. In spite of this and support from the Uxbridge MP Michael Shersby, the station closed in 1988, after serving the town since 1871.

Below: The building remained empty until 1995. The famous 'blue lamp' has gone and the 'acquired' board indicates that it had changed hands. The new owners, the Greene King brewery, then converted it to a pub/restaurant, and named it most appropriately, 'The Old Bill'.

Although there was no reprieve for the old police station, Uxbridge people were relieved when this new, much larger building opened in early 1991 at the High Street end of Harefield Road.

Uxbridge Country Hospital, Harefield Place, in 1976, forty years after its official opening on 7 October 1936. It was originally a seventeenth-century mansion, and was converted from a country club at a cost of £6,000, and used as a convalescent hospital for post-operative cases from Hillingdon Hospital. The hospital was closed in 1968, and Uxbridge Golf Course now occupies the site.

Uxbridge Cottage Hospital, Harefield Road, in March 1930. The hospital had its origins in a smaller building in Park Road that opened in 1868. The Harefield Road building dates from 1914 and was closed in 1978. It has since been used for commercial purposes.

The Isolation Hospital for infectious diseases, Kingston Lane, shortly before its closure in 1984. It was first established in 1882, and extended in 1901 and 1941. The hospital was renamed St John's in 1949. After remaining empty for ten years, the buildings were sold to Brunel University in 1994.

In 1977, this building was all that remained of the former Hillingdon Workhouse, which was built in 1747. In 1930, parts of the workhouse formed the basis of a new hospital originally named Uxbridge County Hospital, and larger wards and nurses' homes were added soon afterwards. By then it had become known as Hillingdon Hospital.

The hospital continued to expand during the 1940s and 1950s, and extra wards in the form of wooden huts sprang up on the opposite side of Pield Heath Road and along Royal Lane. A new maternity wing was added in 1960, followed by a modern ten-storey block in 1967. The picture shows the new building in 1979. Further additions have been made since then.

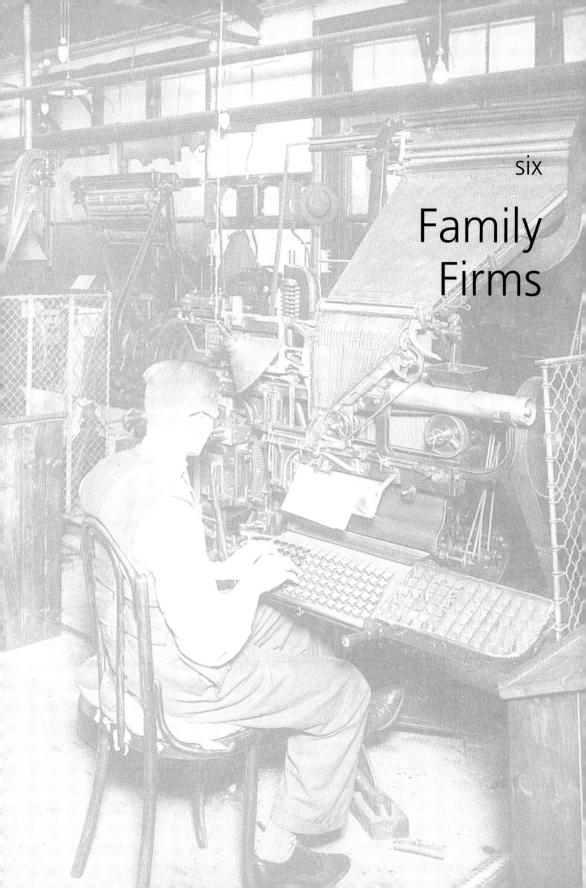

six

Family
Firms

The souvenir brochure produced by Randall's Stores in conjunction with the opening of their new Vine Street building in May 1939. The inside pages advertised dining room suites at 11 guineas (£11.55); three piece suites at 14 guineas (£14.70); and bedroom suites at 18 guineas (£18.90).

The former Randall's building in 1931. The business began when brothers Philip and William Randall from Great Missenden purchased an existing store (Carbutts) in 1888. In due course Philip's son, Albert, took over the business. By the late 1930s, the business had passed to his sons Alec and Norman. Alec's son, John, joined the firm in 1979, became a director in 1981, and Managing Director from 1988 to 1997.

The new, streamlined Randall's building just after its opening in May 1939. The frontage, which is typically 1930s in design, looks similar to cinema architecture of the period with its cream-coloured faience tiling, slimline fin and tower, and canopies. Today the building remains unchanged, except that the clock has long since gone.

One of Randall's delivery vans on Uxbridge Common in the late 1920s, displaying a highly inventive sense of advertising with an exact replica of the Market House on board, complete with appropriate captions.

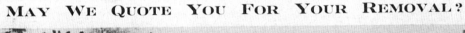

Another enterprising 1920s advertisement for Randall's removal service, which looks to be a vast improvement on their earlier methods of transport – horse and cart. The warehousing referred to on the vans consisted of two large depositories in Lawn Road. The firm also owned a second-hand furniture store on the corner of Chapel Street and Windsor Street.

A view of the baby carriage and nursery furniture department as seen by window shoppers of the 1920s. 'Marmet' prams were on offer from £7 to 9 guineas (£9.45), while a fancy 'Compacta' canopy was under £1.

Since the 1960s, Randall's store has been used as a location for films, television programmes and commercials. Among them were: *Doctor in Love*, *Dixon of Dock Green*, *Z Cars* and *Only Fools and Horses*. In this 1968 picture, Hayley Mills and Hywel Bennett are coming out of the shop, in a scene from *Twisted Nerve*.

Jack Hutton's fish shop and restaurant in Windsor Street. Opened by his wife Ada while Jack was serving abroad in the First World War, it became the first of a chain of thirty-five throughout the area. His three sons, George, Len and Jack, together with daughter Adela, all helped to run the business. By 1988, it was being managed by Adela and her younger brother Len, with the help of two nephews. But then Adela decided that at seventy-five years of age, it was time she retired. Len agreed, and so the business was sold. Their father Jack, senior, who died in 1960, had served: as president of Fassnidge Bowls Club and Ivy Leaf Club, Vice-president of Uxbridge CC and Hayes FC, and on the board of Uxbridge United Charities Trust, in addition to bringing the town its first cinema in 1910.

Mr Jack Hutton and his wife Ada enjoying a family reunion in the early 1950s. Standing, from left to right are George and his wife Mildred, Molly and husband Len, Adela (only daughter) and husband Arthur Harrison, Elizabeth and husband Jack, junior. Sitting are Jack senior and Ada.

A 1930s picture of Kirby Brothers builders' merchants' fleet of vehicles with some of the rapidly increasing staff. The business was established in 1913 when Frank and Robert Kirby opened a small shop at 152 High Street. After serving in the First World War, the brothers moved to a larger shop nearby, with a yard and outbuildings which can be seen in the photograph. Various new premises were acquired throughout the next four decades, with most of them in the High Street. When Frank Kirby died in 1955, the company was employing 173 people. This figure had risen to over 250 by the time Robert Kirby died in 1966. The firm was taken over in 1967 by Mercia Ltd, and on 1 April 1971, the name Kirby Bros finally disappeared.

The Kirby Brothers message/advertisement that appeared in the Uxbridge souvenir programme for the coronation of King George VI and Queen Elizabeth in May 1937.

Suters' Clothing and Drapery store on the corner of High Street and Windsor Street in December 1932. The Suter family – George snr and sons Clarence, George jnr, Frank and John – acquired the premises in 1924 from Carrick and Coles, who had occupied the corner site since 1868, when the building was known as Waterloo House.

Suters' final sale in 1937, after the site had been bought by Montague Burton, who claimed to be the 'world's largest tailoring organisation', and offered men's suits at 45 shillings (£2.25). The building had remained unchanged during the thirteen years of Suters' occupancy.

William Coad's department store or 'Bon Marché' in the High Street, immediately opposite Messrs. Suters, who acquired the shop in 1929. They decided to retain the name Coad until 1937, when they moved across the street, and completely rebuilt the site.

This was the finished article – the result of the rebuilding of Coad's. There is a real Christmassy feel to this December 1937 picture of the new premises. The Christmas trees on the rooftop topped with real snow complete a perfect setting. Next door is the original Woolworth building – the 3d and 6d stores. 'Woolies' sold anything and everything; gramophone records and sheet music cost 6d (2½ pence), and youngsters could even buy a pennyworth of broken biscuits or chocolate. The store is still in place, and completely modernised, but the prices have risen somewhat! In 1978, Suters' business was purchased by Owen Owen.

George Twinn in front of his corn merchants and greengrocery shop at 29 Windsor Street in the early 1920s. He was joined in the business at the end of the First World War by his two sons and two daughters who had all been on war service. George died in 1933, and the family continued the business until it was sold in 1938.

George's son Reginald with his wife Emily, outside their greengrocery shop in The Lynch, in 1979. The shop was converted from the first Uxbridge cinema, Rockingham Hall, after being purchased by the family as a corn store during the 1920s. From 1946, after his release from the Army, Reg and his wife ran the business and a delivery round. His brother had opened a general shop at 38 Rockingham Road in the 1930s.

Sarah Thompson outside her confectionery shop at 167 High Street which she established in 1917. Her son operated a wholesale business from the same address. In 1934, the family moved to newly built premises near the Regal cinema, retaining their trading name of Percy's.

Sarah Thompson in front of her new shop at 236 High Street, where the business was expanded to include tobacco, toys and in particular model railways. It was here that her grandson Tommy joined her and his father on the staff, and, after their deaths he kept the shop going until his retirement in 1983, when the business was sold.

D.C. Grant and Son's jewellers and watchmakers shop at 211 High Street in the late 1950s. Mr Grant established the business after being demobbed from the RAF in 1924, and working for two years in a small shop in Bonny's Market. In 1956, he acquired an adjacent property – the former Black and White Café, which he converted into a watch, clock and repair department, to be run by his son Tony.

Mr Grant stops to smile for the camera, while serving a customer. Behind him stands a grandfather clock, which is priced at £95. He retired in December 1963 after selling the premises to a development company. His son, Tony, carried on the family business at various shops in the town: at Bakers Road, the concourse of the Underground railway station, and in Windsor Street. Now his grandson Lou has taken over, and his shop is back on the High Street, not far from where it all began eighty years ago.

Right: Another 1950s view of Grant's shop. The 'bobby on the beat' outside was a familiar sight in those days and was a considerable deterrent against street crime.

Below: Huge crowds assembling outside J.S. Davy & Son's shop at 18 High Street on Thursday 23 January 1964, which was the opening day of a three-day closing down sale. In the event it ran for only two, because by Saturday morning the shop was almost empty. James Septimus Davy founded the business in 1865, and when he died in 1909, his son Wallace took over. Then when he retired in around 1950, responsibility for the shop and their wholesale operation rested on his sons. Davy's will always be remembered as a high class toy shop and stationers, whose windows invariably displayed working Meccano cranes and lead soldiers, with an extensive model railway layout on the first floor.

Miller's Outfitters, Windsor Street, in the early 1920s. The business was purchased by brothers Rendle and Kenneth Dubrey in 1926. They retained the name Miller's for trading purposes, and Rendle and his family lived in a flat above the shop.

The shop in the mid-1930s with sales assistant Charlie Reynolds outside. An adjacent butcher's shop had its slaughterhouse at the rear of Miller's, and animals were frequently led there through the alleyway dividing the two buildings.

The outfitters had undergone many changes to its frontage as indicated by this picture taken during the 1970s. The gentleman leaning on the shovel is Kenneth Dubrey's son Bob. After Rendle's death, his son Jack took over the running of the business and moved to West Drayton to manage the second Miller's shop, which was opened by his father in 1925. When it closed in 1983, Jack rejoined Bob in their original Windsor Street premises until it too was sold in 1988.

J.R. Palmer's ironmongery shop, on the corner of Windsor Street and Cross Street in the 1930s. The original building was Leno's 6½d Bazaar and then belonged to Grainge's building firm, before being acquired by John Palmer, by which time it had been completely rebuilt. In addition to ironmongery, the shop specialised in fishing rods, air guns, pistols and sheath knives. John Palmer's son, Oswald, had always managed the business, and on his father's death, took it over completely before eventually selling up and moving to Worthing in the 1960s.

Above: The 'Bon Bon' confectionery and tobacco shop in New Windsor Street in the late 1920s. The proprietor's wife, Avis Rashbrook and her daughter May, are standing by the doorway. The shop was like an Aladdin's cave for youngsters, for displayed under the glass counters was an array of goodies, including sherbet fountains, liquorice pipes and bootlaces, gobstoppers, aniseed balls and everlasting strips, with many items priced at a farthing or halfpenny.

Left: A 1928 portrait of the Bon Bon's owner, Charles Ernest Rashbrook. He and his wife ran the shop together, helped occasionally by one of their four daughters. Avis died in 1953, and Charles died two years later in a fire at his home near the shop. By then it had changed hands and was named 'The Cabin'. Later, when it changed hands for a second time, and was renamed 'The News Hut', the original corrugated iron shack-like construction was enlarged and rebuilt in brick. It now trades as a general store and newsagents.

Margaret Walbridge in the doorway of the sweet shop at 39 Windsor Street, which was established by her father Albert Webb in 1933. Albert also ran a kiosk in the Fassnidge Recreation Ground during the 1930s. After her parents death, Margaret ran the Windsor Street shop until 2001, when she retired and disposed of the business. In 1990, the 400-year-old shop was used in an episode of ITV's *Poirot* detective series, *The A.B.C. Murders*.

Newsagent Harry Heasman is with a customer in what remained of his old news stand in the High Street, before the present-day brick building replaced it. Harry first began trading in 1948 from a makeshift wooden shack at the side of Suter's store, and in later years was helped by his son Barry until he left the area. It was then that his daughter-in-law, Wendy, came to help out for a few weeks. That was in 1980, and now, twenty-four years later, she is still there, having managed the business herself for the past ten years.

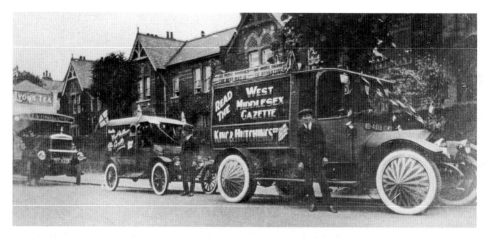

One of King and Hutchings first delivery vans in the early 1920s, not long after the two firms' merger in 1919. Tobacconist and printer, John King, had established the *Uxbridge Gazette* in 1880 in opposition to the *Buckinghamshire Advertiser* which originated in 1840, when it was known as *Broadwater's Journal*. The *Journal* was acquired by Walter Hutchings in 1903. John King died in 1912 and Walter Hutchings in 1917, so neither saw the amalgamation. King's High Street printing works had been destroyed in a fire, so the partnership began in Hutchings's works in Cricketfield Road, and the newspaper became the *Middlesex Advertiser and County Gazette*.

Gazette compositors at work on their machines in the early 1930s. By now the 'family firm' was being managed by John King's sons, Charles and John, along with Howard and Leonard Hutchings, who were the brothers of Walter. The editor was Harry Hamson, who had been appointed in 1906 by Walter, and held the position until his retirement in 1946.

A more modern type of delivery van used by the newspaper in the late 1940s.

King and Hutchings printing plant, and at one time editorial offices, in Cricketfield Road. The firm was now producing 500,000 newspapers a week, and had built another, much larger set of offices and printing works on the opposite side of the road. It happened fortuitously, as the buildings pictured were destroyed in a devastating fire in January 1968.

Some of the 300 employees from various branches of King and Hutchings at a celebratory dinner dance held at Lyons Corner House, Coventry Street in October 1951. The company now had offices in Harrow, Wembley, Ealing, Acton, Southall and Amersham. The function was attended by John S. King, who had given over forty years' service to the firm, and J.H.J. Hutchings, son of Howard. Chairman of the board, C.E. King, JP, (forty-three years with the company) was unable to attend due to ill health, but sent a message in which he described the firm as 'a happy family business with many employees having at least forty years' service'.

Gazette staff at their Bakers Road offices in April 2002, proudly displaying the 'Best News Pages' trophy, which was awarded by the papers new owners Trinity Mirror Group. The picture shows current editor, Adrian Seal, holding the certificate, and former editor, Anthony Longden, with the trophy. Anthony edited the paper for eight years.

seven

Events and Personalities

Marathon running appeared to be the 'in thing' in 1908, after the Olympic runners had passed through Uxbridge on their way to White City, where the Games were held that year. On 26 August, the town organised its own version in the form of a boys' round-the-town race, and here the competitors anxiously await the 'off', outside the George Inn in the High Street. Forty years on, the Olympic flame was carried through Uxbridge on 29 July 1948, en route from Dover to Wembley Stadium.

A welcoming party at Belmont Road Metropolitan Station on 9 July 1929, for the lady librarian, Mrs Sprague from Uxbridge, Massachusetts. The party included J. Cochrane, C.E. King, Revd F. Riches Lowe, H. Knight and G. Crook. Before the days of 'town twinning', Uxbridge always had a close rapport with its American namesake, and reciprocal visits were often made between the two towns.

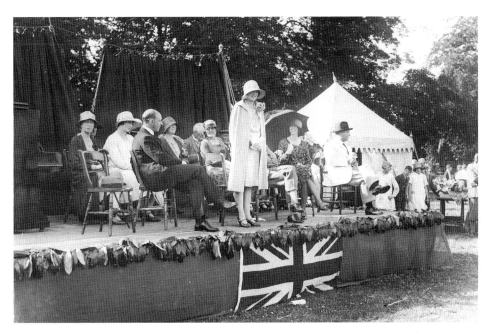

Lady Ossulston opening the Uxbridge Conservatives' Fête on 11 July 1928, held in the
grounds of The Hermitage, Belmont Road. Seated on the left is Commander C.D. Burney,
MP, who, with a General Election scheduled for May 1929, took the opportunity of making
a political speech.

Mrs Kate Fassnidge opening a garden fête in the grounds of her home, 'The Cedars', High
Street, in July 1929. The proceeds went to Dr Barnardo's Homes. Mrs Fassnidge was a great
benefactress to the town, and bequeathed her house and gardens to Uxbridge council.

Left and below: Pictures that featured in the Uxbridge souvenir brochure produced for the coronation of King George VI and Queen Elizabeth on 12 May 1937. The town celebrated the event in great style with a 'Grand Procession' from the High Street to the Show Ground in Park Road. The Uxbridge and Hillingdon Prize Band, the Dagenham Girl Pipers and the Carnival Queen Joan Price, with her Maids of Honour were all in attendance. In the evening, a second (torchlight) procession starting from the swimming pool, made a tour of the town's main streets, and the celebrations culminated with a firework display and mammoth bonfire on Uxbridge Common. A film was made of the day's events and was shown at the Regal cinema during the following week.

Uxbridge Coronation Festivities 1937

Miss IRENE HARRIS

Miss EDITH LOWE

Miss M. SEARLE

Miss D. J. COOPER

Miss PEGGY FOSTER

Miss IVY KILBEY

MAIDS OF HONOUR

Opposite below: The No.1 RAF Dance Orchestra, the 'Squadronaires', known to their fans as the 'Squads'. Formed at Uxbridge in 1940, at the instigation of the RAF's Director of Music, Wing Commander R.P. O'Donnell, the personnel included top musicians from the big name bands of the day. Led by Sgt Jimmy Miller (second from left), the line-up featured trumpeters Kenny Baker and Tommy McQuator, clarinettists Andy McDevitt (second from right) and Jimmy Durante, pianist Ronnie Aldrich, drummer Jock Cummings, guitarist Sid Colin (on extreme left) and trombonist George Chisholm (in back row). Based at Uxbridge for the duration, the band toured military bases and variety theatres. They made radio broadcasts and played at charity concerts, with two of them being at the Odeon cinema. Their distinctive signature tune 'There's Something in the Air' became well known, and eventually the 'Squadronaires' were considered the best British swing band of the war.

Stage and screen star Sir Laurence Olivier opening a fête in aid of the Red Cross Sick and Wounded Fund at Old Vine Cottage, Cowley on 15 July 1944. Hosts Mr and Mrs W.S. Try provided the venue for the event, which was attended by over 2,000 people and raised £750 for the charity. Sir Laurence helped by selling autographs for one shilling (5p) each.

When the Second World War ended on 7 May 1945, the next day was designated as VE Day, and celebrations began nationwide. A two-day national holiday was declared and countless street parties were organised in every town and village. This group of children and adults from the Uxbridge Moor area are enjoying the festivities at St John's Hall, which was built opposite the church in April 1932.

Part of the Victory Parade marching through the High Street on a wet Saturday on 8 June 1946. Although the end of the Second World War came on 14 August 1945, the celebrations had been postponed. The procession was on its way to the swimming school car park where a service of dedication and remembrance was held. The day ended with the customary torchlight procession to the Common, followed by the lighting of a bonfire and a firework display. The 'Victory Queen' was Olive Walling who, as Olive Maunder, had been the Beauty Queen of 1944.

The Uxbridge Show committee and officials at the showground at Park Road on 1 August 1948. Instituted in 1909 as a Horticultural, then Agricultural Show, this annual Bank Holiday event expanded throughout the twentieth century to embrace a much wider range of activities, and in 1938 was attended by 20,000 people. Notable personalities in the front row include: council Chairman W.E. Black, JP, W.S. Try and E. Chaney who presented the prizes. The event was renamed Hillingdon Show in 1966, and has been known as the Middlesex Show since 1986.

A group participating in a 'Brains Trust' programme at the Regal cinema on 8 June 1951 in connection with Uxbridge Road Courtesy Week. From left to right are: Councillors S.L. Meggeson, N. Holland, J. Poole, S.C. Clifton, radio celebrity Anona Wynn (question master), Charles Curran MP and Regal manager W. Linsell.

On 3 November 1952, Uxbridge people may have been surprised to see two veteran cars being driven around the town by the well-known film stars, Kenneth More, Kay Kendall, John Gregson and Dinah Sheridan. They were filming the classic British comedy, *Genevieve*, and are seen here in Chapel Street at F. & V. Payne's hardware shop (formerly J. Leno's). The cars were loaned to the film company by Norman Reeves (Motors) Ltd, which was founded in the 1920s. Both Mr Reeves and his son Norman jnr were veteran car enthusiasts. The vehicle on the left acting as Genevieve is a Darracq.

Another Norman Reeves veteran car taking part in an Argosy Players pageant on June 28 1953, as part of Coronation Year celebrations. Group members attired in costumes from the fifteenth century to the present day are seen leaving for St Andrew's Church Fête, after staging a display at Hillingdon Church Garden Party.

To mark the fiftieth anniversary of the Metropolitan line's extension to Uxbridge, a 'Jubilee Special' excursion was arranged by railway enthusiast Peter Grace. On 4 July 1954, London Transport's oldest steam train, a fifty-eight-year-old locomotive engine No.L44, carried 290 passengers from Baker Street to Uxbridge Underground station in a journey time of forty-one minutes at a special price of 5s (25p) each. The picture shows the train being greeted by members of Argosy Players dressed as Edwardians.

Once again Uxbridge is used as a location for a British film. This time it is the GWR station in Vine Street, which was previously seen in a 1948 film *Trottie True*. The picture shows Bill Travers and Virginia McKenna, on 17 August 1956, about to begin a scene in *The Smallest Show On Earth* starring Peter Sellers. Shepperton Studios had chosen the station to represent 'a dreary little Midlands station', and may have been influenced by Uxbridge Chamber of Trade's remarks earlier in the year, when they described it as 'dirty, dilapidated and a disgrace.'

HRH the Duchess of Kent, her daughter Princess Alexandra, and son the Duke of Kent walking along the High Street on Uxbridge 'Charter Day'on 18 May 1955. At a special ceremony in the Regal cinema, the Duchess formally handed over the Charter granting the town borough status.

Officials and spectators assembled outside the RAF station on 16 December 1957 to witness the official opening of the imposing St Andrew's Gate which was constructed to replace the original wooden one erected in 1919. Group Captain F.W. Stannard, the Station Commander, is seen addressing the assembly prior to the unlocking of the two gates by the Mayor, Alderman S.L. Meggeson (in the foreground). Distinguished guests included: the Inspector General of the RAF Air Marshal Sir Walter Dawson, Frank Beswick, MP, and Sir Frederick Handley Page CBE, the Lord Lieutenant of the County of Middlesex. The left-hand gate bears the coat of arms of the borough of Uxbridge, and the RAF Uxbridge badge is on the right.

HRH the Duchess of Kent on a conducted tour of Hillingdon Hospital on 5 July 1960, prior to officially opening the new maternity wing named after her. In the background are some of the 'temporary' huts that had served as wards for many years. The new block, which had cost £300,000, was dedicated by the Bishop of Kensington. Before the Duchess left, she was presented with a farewell gift by nine-year-old Joyce Frankenberg, the daughter of the senior gynaecologist, John Frankenberg. Joyce grew up to become film actress Jane Seymour.

The band of the WRAF taking part in a Freedom of the Borough parade, c.1974, led by Flight Lieutenant, R. Thompsett, Director of Music. Because of the close ties between the town and the RAF since 1917, the station was granted the Freedom of the Borough of Uxbridge on 19 March 1960. It entitled them to march through the streets of Uxbridge on ceremonial occasions with 'drums beating, bands playing, colours flying, swords drawn and bayonets fixed'.

Another RAF parade through the town on 18 May 1977. This time it was to mark the sixtieth anniversary of the opening of the depot. Senior Drum Major of the RAF, Flight Sergeant T. McCarthy, leads the Central Band through historic Windsor Street, followed by the Queen's Colour Squadron and 200 airmen and airwomen.

It's 'eyes right' as the Queen's Colour Squadron receives the 'hat to shoulder' salute from the Mayor, as the parade moves through the High Street on its way to Windsor Street. The sixtieth anniversary march started from St Andrew's Gate and returned to the camp via Vine Street.

Former Uxbridge cricket captain, Mike Stoneman, landlord of the Red Lion Inn, Hillingdon Village, from 1978 to 1998 and his wife Val, prior to leaving for Ascot Races on 19 June 1985, with a party of friends and customers. The sixteenth-century inn is noted for a visit by King Charles I in April 1646. The King and his chaplain had escaped from Oxford, and were en route for London before going on to Newark to join the Scottish army.

The RAF Central Band at the launch of a new CD, *Salute to Heroes,* on 21 June 1990. The band was formed in 1920, and has travelled millions of miles around the world from its permanent home in Uxbridge. The aircraft in the background situated just inside the main gates, is a replica of a Mark 9 Spitfire, as flown by 64 Squadron from Hornchurch in 1942.

HRH Prince Edward visited RAF Uxbridge on 20 February 1991 and is seen here talking to the families of airmen and airwomen serving in the Gulf War. Accompanied by his equerry, Lieutenant Sean O'Dwyer, he was then entertained in the Officers' Mess by the Station Commander, Group Captain Ray Hart.

Her Majesty the Queen's visit on 25 June 2002 was a momentous moment in the history of Uxbridge. The Queen, accompanied by Prince Philip, had been invited to unveil a statue opposite the Market House, as part of her Golden Jubilee Tour of outer London Boroughs. The sculpture, titled 'Anticipation', created by Anita Lafford, had been commissioned by the Hillingdon Arts Association, and was funded entirely by voluntary contributions. The Queen is seen here with the Mayor, Councillor Josephine Barrett, after the ceremony, witnessed by several thousand spectators.

Bernard Miles as the hunchback Richard III with the two 'princes in the tower', in an Uxbridge County School production of Shakespeare's play in 1926. Bernard was born at New Road, Hillingdon, on 27 September 1907, and while still at school was inspired by drama teacher, Cecilia Hill, to make the stage his career. After leaving Pembroke College, Oxford, he made his professional debut in *Richard III* – not in the lead, however, but as a messenger. In 1932, he began a second career in films, and during the Second World War scored notable successes in *Quiet Wedding*, *In Which We Serve* and *One of Our Aircraft is Missing* among many others. He continued to appear at the 'Old Vic' during the 1940s, and after six years of planning, founded the Mermaid Theatre at Puddle Dock in 1959. Bernard was created CBE in 1953, knighted in 1969, and made a life peer in 1979 – as Lord Miles of Blackfriars in the City of London.

Bernard Miles photographed on a return visit to Hillingdon in April 1986. His wife, the actress Josephine Wilson, died in 1990, and shortly afterwards Bernard died on 14 June 1991, leaving a son and daughter.

Arthur William Kingston, who lived at Willowbank, Denham, from 1945 until his death on 27 June 1974. Arthur was a research engineer, inventor and a pioneer of moving pictures. After working as a newsreel cameraman with Pathé Frères in London, he joined the Royal Flying Corps School of Photography. Among his many inventions in the field of cinema and still photography, the greatest was the plastic lens, which he patented in 1934. Earlier, he had made significant experiments with sound projection, and shot the first sound documentary about the Antarctic explorer, Ernest Shackleton. Already a Fellow of the British Kinematographic Society, he was elected a Fellow of the Royal Photographic Society in 1967.

Betty Ella Kingston (née Giles) married Arthur Kingston in 1945. They met during the Second World War, while she was serving in the Women's Auxiliary Air Force at RAF Uxbridge. Betty enlisted in 1940, and was soon working in the underground Operations Room of Headquarters No.11 Group, Fighter Command. She spent the whole of the war doing this job, being particularly vital during the Battle of Britain, and was eventually promoted to sergeant in charge of one of the watches. It was here that she had the privilege of meeting Queen Elizabeth during one of her visits with King George VI in 1940/1941. From the 1970s, Betty served on the committee of Uxbridge History Society for twenty-five years, and was then granted life membership. She died on 22 August 2002, leaving a married daughter.

Uxbridge MP, John Randall, demonstrating a mangle that is a relic of the type sold by his family firm, Randall's Stores, in the 1930s. John is the great-grandson of the founder of the business, Philip Randall, and joined the firm in 1979. John was a former treasurer and chairman of Uxbridge Conservative Association, and was chosen to stand as their Parliamentary candidate following the death of his friend, Sir Michael Shersby, in 1997. He was elected, and so relinquished his position as Managing Director of Randall's, which he had held from 1988. His spare time (when he gets any) is devoted to his main hobby, ornithology.

The late Mark McManus at St Mary's RC School reunion in March 1990, with two of his former teachers, Madge Daly and Molly Duffy. Sisters Madge and Molly had joined the staff of the Rockingham Road school during the 1930s. The lady on the extreme left is another long-serving teacher, Ina Jubb. Mark attended St Mary's during the 1950s, and emigrated to Australia in 1963. Eventually he achieved world-wide fame in the television series, *Taggart*, over a period of eleven years. He died on 6 June 1994, after a succession of personal tragedies.

A happy reunion of the Frankenberg family in 1988. From left to right: Mieke, Jane Seymour (formerly Joyce Frankenberg), Anne, Sally and John. After serving in the RAF during the Second World War, John Frankenberg joined Hillingdon Hospital gynaecological staff as a houseman in 1946. Following a brief spell at hospitals in London, he returned to Hillingdon in 1953 as a registrar, eventually progressing to senior registrar and consultant. While there, he designed and developed many inventions, which were subsequently adopted by other hospitals in their maternity departments. John, who retired in 1979 and died in 1990, married Mieke (who had spent three years in a Japanese POW camp during the Second World War) in 1950. Jane Seymour has made over fifty films including *Live and Let Die*, *Young Winston*, *The Four Feathers* and *Battlestar Galactica*. Now a successful author and painter, she was awarded the OBE in 2000, in recognition of her work for various charities. She is married to director James Keach.

The Uxbridge historian, Ken Pearce, in a pensive mood outside the Crown and Treaty in 1992. Known locally as the Old Treaty House, the inn dates from the sixteenth century, and in 1645 was the venue for negotiations between the Royalists and Parliamentarians in a bid to end the Civil War. The talks broke down and no treaty was signed, but the inn's title remained.

Chris Wren sitting in the chair used by Winston Churchill in the underground Operations Room at RAF Uxbridge, during the Battle of Britain. During the Second World War, the 'bunker' was twice visited by King George VI and Queen Elizabeth, Lord Mountbatten, and Field Marshal Montgomery and Generals Eisenhower and de Gaulle. After a career in the RAF spanning thirty-seven years, ex-Warrant Officer Chris Wren was appointed civilian curator of the underground museum, which is visited by 8,000 people each year. Chris conducts them on tours that include the plotting room (preserved as it was in 1940) and six rooms of wartime memorabilia. He concludes with a superb thirty-minute summary of the six-year-long war.

The celebrated astrologer and television presenter, Russell Grant, returned to his home town in August 1999, to film scenes for his TV series, *Russell Grant's Postcards*. He included: Webb's sweet shop, St Margaret's Church and the Crown and Treaty Inn. Russell lived in and around Uxbridge for many years, and still retains his interest in the district. He is president of the Uxbridge History Society, and is continually campaigning to keep the name of the historic county of Middlesex alive.

Other local titles published by Tempus

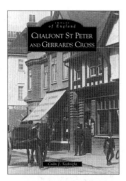

Chalfont St Peter and Gerrards Cross
COLIN J. SEABRIGHT

This volume captures the twentieth-century history of two adjacent villages –
from the shops and businesses that evolved from the market village of Chalfont
St Peter, to the rapid development of Gerrards Cross into a commuter village.
This book documents scenes which will appeal to those who have known the
area and to those who now live in this historically interesting region.
0 7524 2493 9

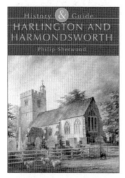

Harlington and Harmondsworth History and Guide
PHILIP SHERWOOD

This book deals with the history of the two parishes of Harlington and
Harmondsworth, from when they first appeared in written records in the
ninth century, up to the present day. The book includes a walking tour of the
town which can be used independently of the main text of the book and
enables the reader to embark on a journey into the areas past through its
existing streets and buildings.
0 7524 2609 5

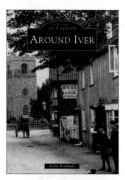

Around Iver
STELLA ROWLANDS

Once surrounded by fields, the villages of Iver, Iver Heath and Richings Park
have seen many changes over the last century. With 230 old pictures, this
collection visits the cottage hospital, country houses, churches, schools,
streets, and recalls the events and celebrations, as well as local characters.
Accompanied by informative text, *Around Iver* will reawaken nostalgic
memories for some, while offering a unique glimpse of the past for others.
0 7524 2862 4

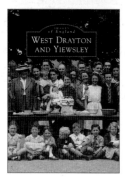

West Drayton and Yiewsley
JAMES SKINNER

This compilation of over 200 old photographs illustrates the history of the two
Middlesex towns of West Drayton and Yiewsley, charting their progress from
agricultural communities of golden cornfields, to the coming of the railway and
the growth of industry, including brickmaking, gravel and ballast
production. With chapters covering all aspects of life, from school, religion and
work to sport, recreation and music, this volume serves as a valuable record of
life gone by, and will delight both long-term residents and newcomers alike.
0 7524 2841 1

If you are interested in purchasing other books published by Tempus, or in case you have difficulty finding any
Tempus books in your local bookshop, you can also place orders directly through our website

www.tempus-publishing.com

or from **BOOKPOST**, Freepost, PO Box 29, Douglas, Isle of Man, IM99 1BQ
tel 01624 836000 email bookshop@enterprise.net